SUPER STARS!
TIMES TABLES
Activity Book

ARCTURUS

ARCTURUS

This edition published in 2019 by Arcturus Publishing Limited
26/27 Bickels Yard, 151–153 Bermondsey Street,
London SE1 3HA

Written by Lorenzo McLellan
Illustrated by Natasha Rimmington
Designed by Well Nice
Edited by Sebastian Rydberg

ISBN: 978-1-78950-025-7
CH006146NT
Supplier 29, Date 0219, Print run 7925

Printed in China

How to Use This Book

Welcome to the world of Super Stars! This book is filled with times tables facts to help you learn the basics of multiplying and dividing—all while having fun!

Read about each new topic before you dive in to the activities.

Test your knowledge with exciting activities throughout.

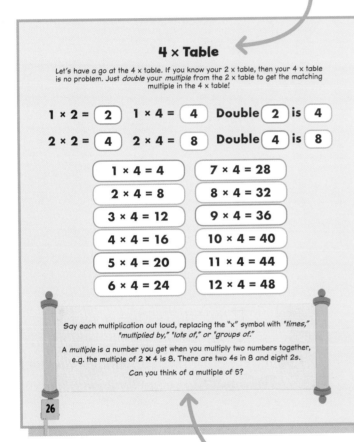

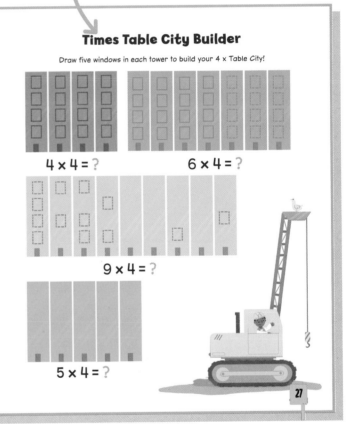

All new topics come with practice activities to learn key skills.

Learn the Symbols (× ÷ =)

To start multiplying and dividing, these are the symbols you'll need to know.

×

"TIMES," "MULTIPLIED BY," "LOTS OF," OR "GROUPS OF"

÷

"DIVIDED BY" OR "GROUPING"

=

"IS EQUAL TO"

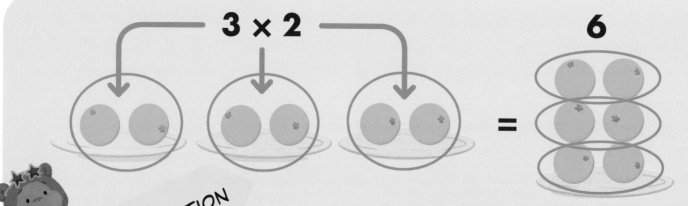

3 × 2

6

=

MULTIPLICATION

Here we have 3 **groups of** 2 oranges, which is equal to 6 oranges. 3 **multiplied by** 2 is equal to 6.

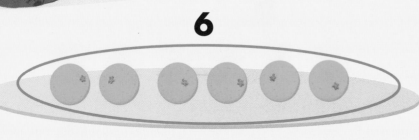

6

Division is the opposite of multiplication. To share 6 oranges equally, you need to divide them. 6 oranges **divided by** 3 is equal to 2 oranges.

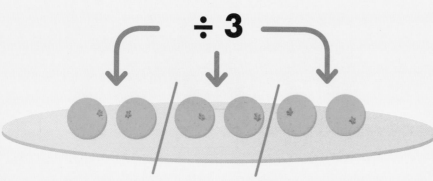

÷ 3

= 2

DIVISION

Pick the correct symbol to make the number sentence correct.

2 ? 4 = 8

× or ÷

8 ? 2 = 4

× or ÷

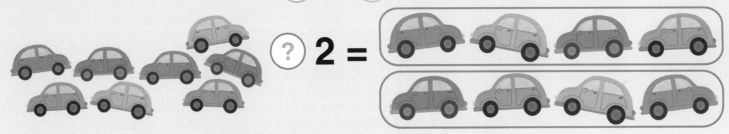

Machine Mix-up

Help the robot sort the words and phrases into the correct operation machine.

MULTIPLICATION

1
2
3
4

DIVIDED BY

MULTIPLIED BY

GROUPING

SHARING

GROUPS OF

TIMES

LOTS OF

DIVISION

1

2

3

Multiplication: Repeated Addition

When we use multiplication, we are simply doing *repeated addition*.
3 x 2 = 6 is the same as 2 + 2 + 2 = 6.

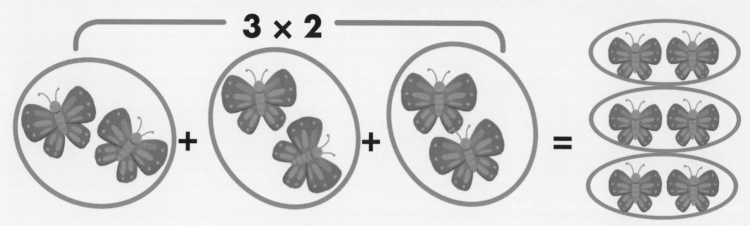

3 × 2

Here is another way of showing repeated addition. It's called a bar model.

6		
2	2	2

Missing Numbers

Rewrite this multiplication as repeated addition.
Add the correct amounts of fish.

4 × 2 = 8

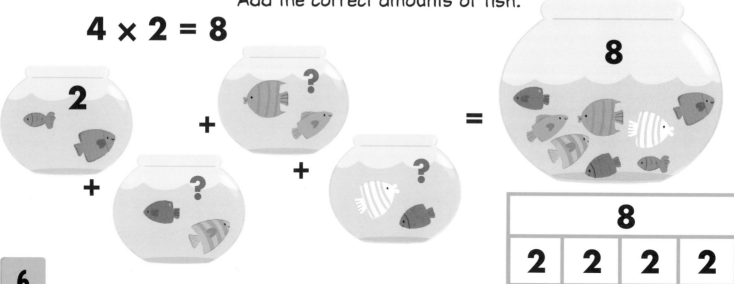

8			
2	2	2	2

Monkey Match Up

Draw a line to match each multiplication to the correct repeated addition and bar model?

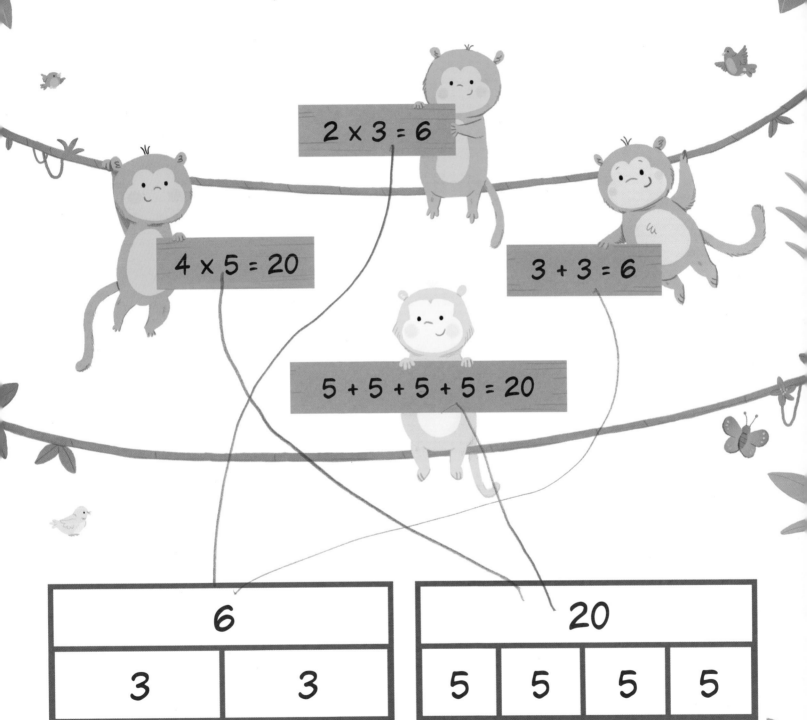

2 x 3 = 6

4 x 5 = 20

3 + 3 = 6

5 + 5 + 5 + 5 = 20

6	
3	3

20			
5	5	5	5

10 × Table

Let's start learning our times tables. We will begin with our 10 x table.

1 × 10 = 10

2 × 10 = 20

3 × 10 = 30

4 × 10 = 40

5 × 10 = 50

6 × 10 = 60

7 × 10 = 70

8 × 10 = 80

9 × 10 = 90

10 × 10 = 100

11 × 10 = 110

12 × 10 = 120

Say each multiplication out loud, replacing the "x" symbol with "times," "multiplied by," "lots of," or "groups of."

Times Table City Builder

Draw ten windows in each tower to build your 10 x Table City!

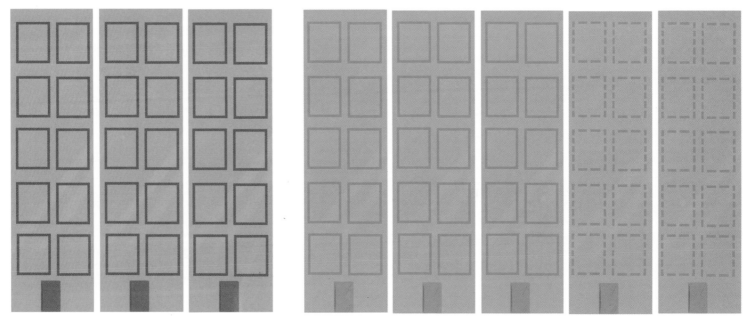

3 x 10 = ? 30

5 x 10 = ? 50

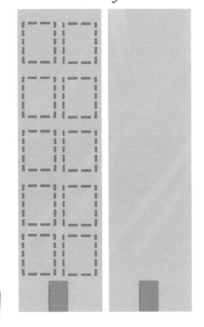

2 x 10 = ? 20

4 x 10 = ? 40

Missing Marbles

Draw in the missing marbles to make bags of 10.

$$3 \times 10 = 30$$

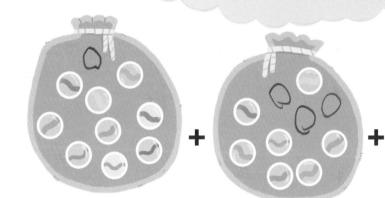 +  =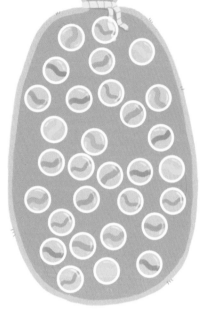

Seal Conceal

Which numbers are the seals hiding?

$2 \times 10 = 20$

$12 \times 10 = 120$

$4 \times 10 = 40$

Wild, Wild West

Match each cowboy with the correct horse.

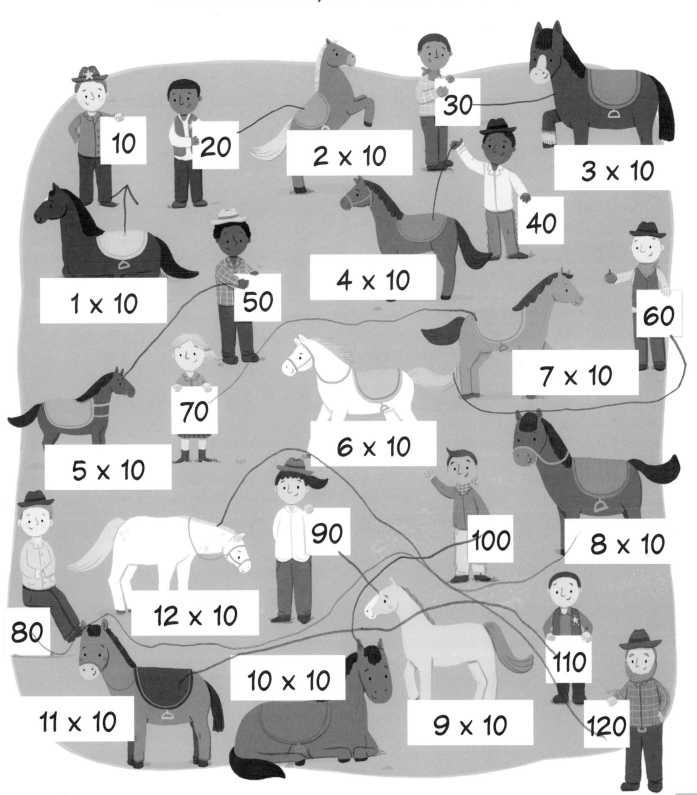

2 × Table

Now let's try learning our 2 x table.

1 × 2 = 2	**7 × 2 = 14**
2 × 2 = 4	**8 × 2 = 16**
3 × 2 = 6	**9 × 2 = 18**
4 × 2 = 8	**10 × 2 = 20**
5 × 2 = 10	**11 × 2 = 22**
6 × 2 = 12	**12 × 2 = 24**

Say each multiplication out loud, replacing the "x" symbol with "times," "multiplied by," "lots of," or "groups of."

Busy Bugs

Make sure each bug has the correct number of spots and work out the answer to each equation.

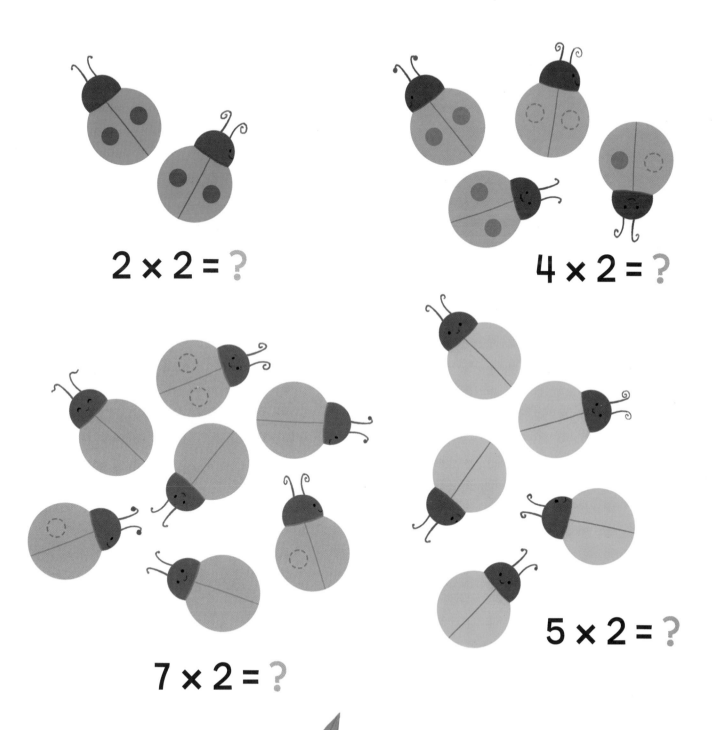

$2 \times 2 = ?$

$4 \times 2 = ?$

$7 \times 2 = ?$

$5 \times 2 = ?$

Pixie Party

Which number is hidden behind each pixie?

$5 \times$  $= 10$

$\times 2 = 20$

$9 \times 2 =$

Spot the Mistake

Circle the egg that is not needed to match the number sentence.

$4 \times 2 = 8$

Superhero Sort Out

Match each superhero to their cape.

15

5 × Table

Now you're ready for your 5 × table.

1 × 5 = 5	**7 × 5 = 35**
2 × 5 = 10	**8 × 5 = 40**
3 × 5 = 15	**9 × 5 = 45**
4 × 5 = 20	**10 × 5 = 50**
5 × 5 = 25	**11 × 5 = 55**
6 × 5 = 30	**12 × 5 = 60**

Say each multiplication out loud, replacing the "×" symbol with "times," "multiplied by," "lots of," or "groups of."

Fish Fill

Make sure there are the right number of fish in
each bowl to work out the correct answer!

$$6 \times 5 = ?$$

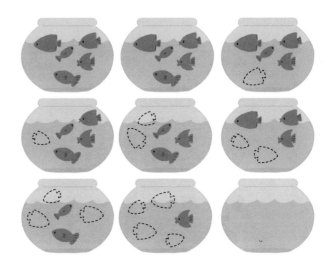

$$9 \times 5 = ?$$

$$5 \times 5 = ?$$

$$7 \times 5 = ?$$

Safari Sun

Which animal has the correct answer?

$5 \times 5 =$

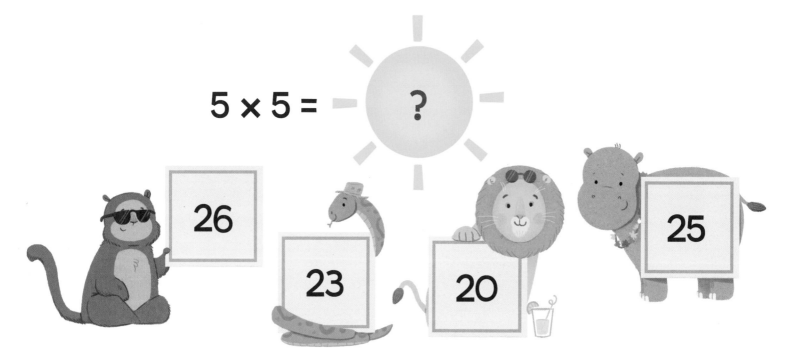

Balloon Brigade

Which numbers are covered by clouds?

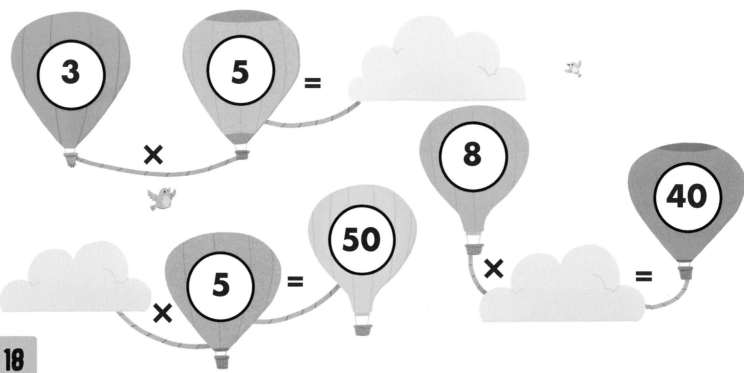

Showtime

Help the clown get to the stage in time for the show!

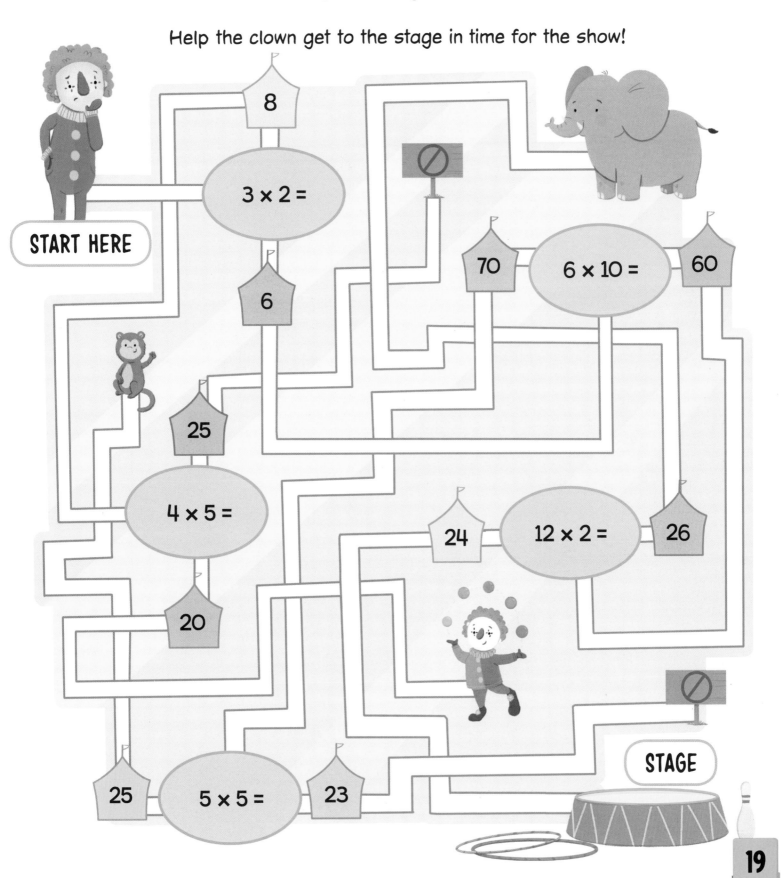

START HERE

8

3 × 2 =

6

70   6 × 10 =   60

25

4 × 5 =

24   12 × 2 =   26

20

25   5 × 5 =   23

STAGE

19

Test Your Knowledge

1) 2 x 2 = ?

2) 3 x 2 = ?

3) 4 x 5 = ?

4) 5 x 5 = ?

5) 6 x 10 = ?

6) 7 x 10 = ?

7) 10 x 10 = ?

8) 11 x 10 = ?

9) 12 x 10 = ?

10) 1 x 10 = ?

Test Your Knowledge

1) 6 x 2 = ?

2) 9 x 2 = ?

3) 2 x 5 = ?

4) 7 x 5 = ?

5) 4 x 10 = ?

6) 9 x 10 = ?

7) 3 x 10 = ?

8) 2 x 10 = ?

9) 12 x 2 = ?

10) 11 x 5 = ?

Multiplication Works Both Ways!

Multiplication is *commutative*. This means that you can swap the numbers you are multiplying around and you still get the same answer!

2 × 5 = 10

5 × 2 = 10

2 × 5 = 10

5 × 2 = 10

Goblin Gruel

Which number is covered by the gruel?

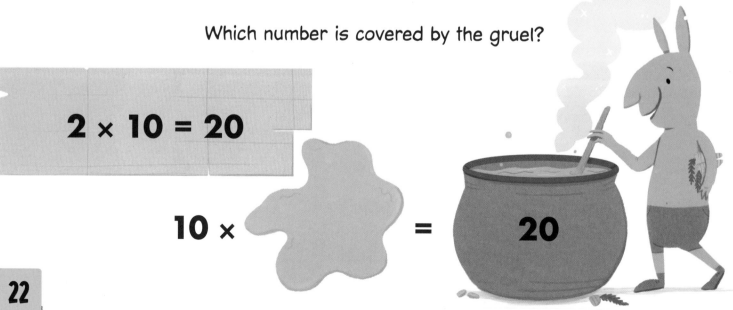

2 × 10 = 20

10 × = 20

22

Hop to It!

Help each frog find its lily pad.

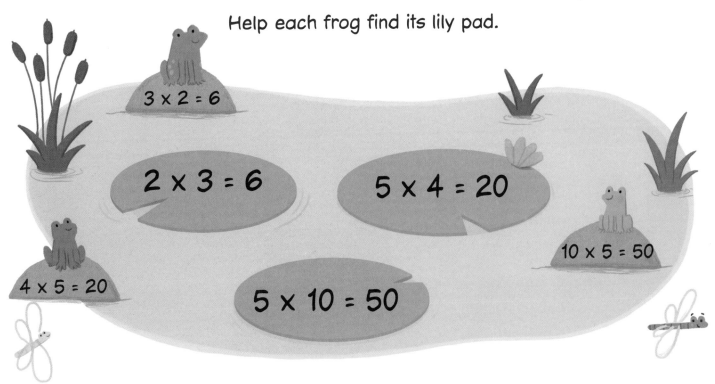

$3 \times 2 = 6$

$2 \times 3 = 6$

$5 \times 4 = 20$

$10 \times 5 = 50$

$4 \times 5 = 20$

$5 \times 10 = 50$

Number Machine

Rewrite each multiplication by swapping around the numbers you're multiplying together.

$3 \times 4 = 12$

$4 \times \_ = 12$

$2 \times 7 = 14$

$\_ \times 2 = 14$

$6 \times 5 = 30$

$\_ \times \_ = 30$

Fish Fun

Draw the groups of fish to show each multiplication.

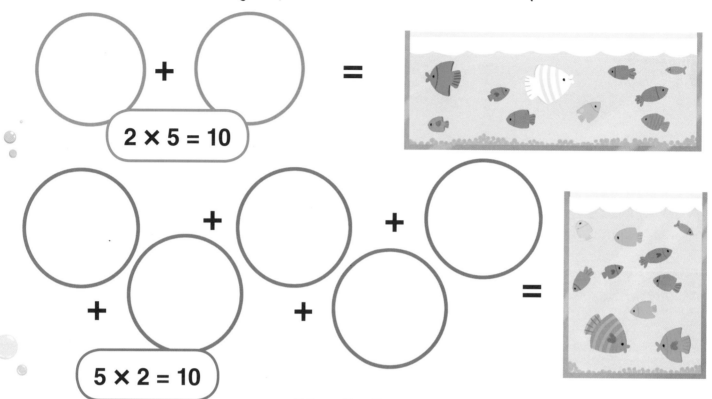

$2 \times 5 = 10$

$5 \times 2 = 10$

Hat Swap

Draw the groups of hats to show each multiplication.

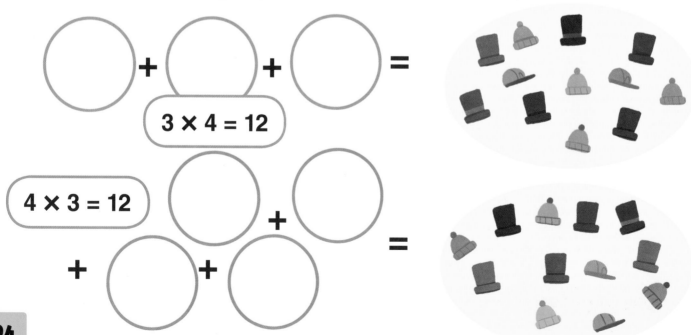

$3 \times 4 = 12$

$4 \times 3 = 12$

Pirate Portrait

Solve the multiplications below and use the key to fill in the pirate.

6 x 2 = ?   5 x 5 = ?   10 x ? = 20   ? x 2 = 12   12 x 5 = ?

4 × Table

Let's have a go at the 4 x table. If you know your 2 x table, then your 4 x table is no problem. Just *double* your *multiple* from the 2 x table to get the matching multiple in the 4 x table!

$1 \times 2 =$ (2) $1 \times 4 =$ (4)   **Double** (2) **is** (4)

$2 \times 2 =$ (4) $2 \times 4 =$ (8)   **Double** (4) **is** (8)

$1 \times 4 = 4$	$7 \times 4 = 28$
$2 \times 4 = 8$	$8 \times 4 = 32$
$3 \times 4 = 12$	$9 \times 4 = 36$
$4 \times 4 = 16$	$10 \times 4 = 40$
$5 \times 4 = 20$	$11 \times 4 = 44$
$6 \times 4 = 24$	$12 \times 4 = 48$

Say each multiplication out loud, replacing the "x" symbol with "times," "multiplied by," "lots of," or "groups of."

A *multiple* is a number you get when you multiply two numbers together, e.g. the multiple of 2 x 4 is 8. There are two 4s in 8 and eight 2s.

Can you think of a multiple of 5?

Times Table City Builder

Draw five windows in each tower to build your 4 x Table City!

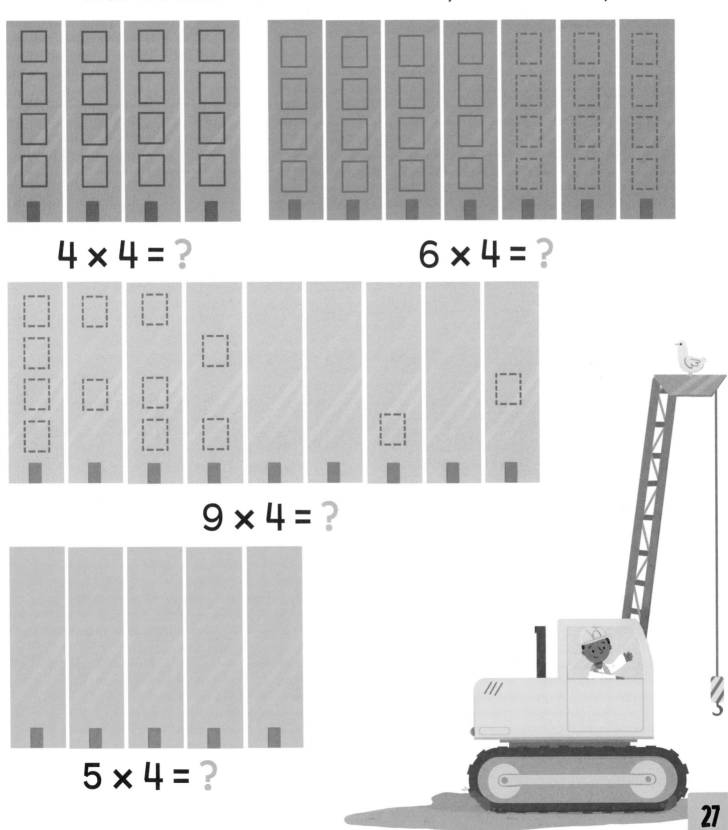

$4 \times 4 = ?$

$6 \times 4 = ?$

$9 \times 4 = ?$

$5 \times 4 = ?$

Dino Dinner

Write the multiplication that matches the picture and work out how many dinosaurs are coming to dinner!

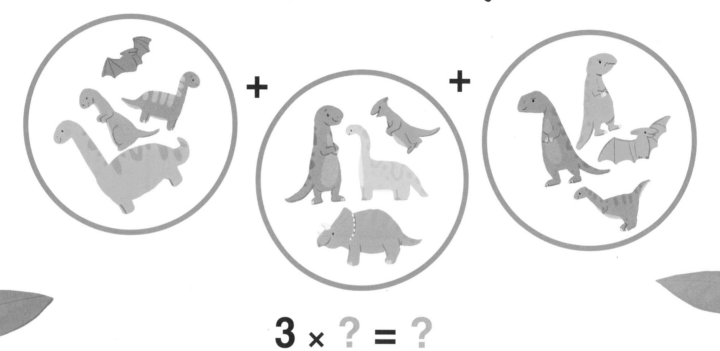

$$3 \times ? = ?$$

Under the Sea

Help the crab find the right shell by solving the multiplication.

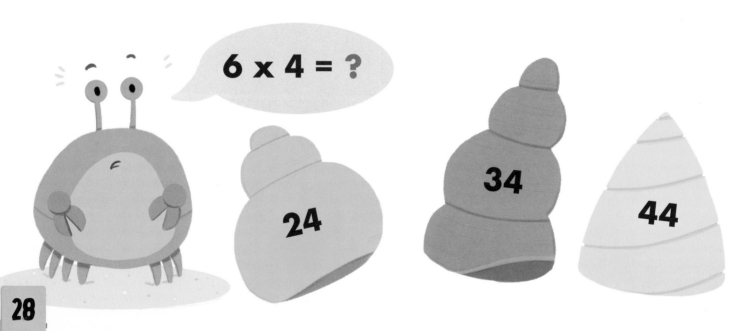

$$6 \times 4 = ?$$

24

34

44

Knight Time!

Fill in the knight's shield by using the key below.

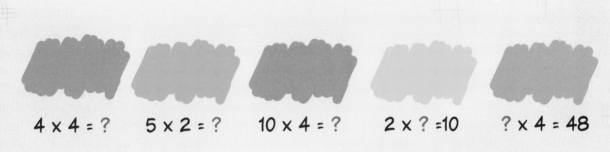

4 x 4 = ?   5 x 2 = ?   10 x 4 = ?   2 x ? = 10   ? x 4 = 48

8 × Table

If you know your 4 x table, then the 8 x table is easy.
Just *double* your *multiple* from the 4 x table to get
the matching multiple in the 8 x table!

$1 \times 4 =$ (4) $1 \times 8 =$ (8)   **Double** (4) **is** (8)

$2 \times 4 =$ (8) $2 \times 8 =$ (16)   **Double** (8) **is** (16)

$1 \times 8 = 8$	$7 \times 8 = 56$
$2 \times 8 = 16$	$8 \times 8 = 64$
$3 \times 8 = 24$	$9 \times 8 = 72$
$4 \times 8 = 32$	$10 \times 8 = 80$
$5 \times 8 = 40$	$11 \times 8 = 88$
$6 \times 8 = 48$	$12 \times 8 = 96$

Say each multiplication out loud, replacing the "x"
symbol with "times," "multiplied by," "lots of," or
"groups of."

Busy Bugs

Make sure each bug has the correct number of spots and work out the answer to each multiplication.

$2 \times 8 = ?$

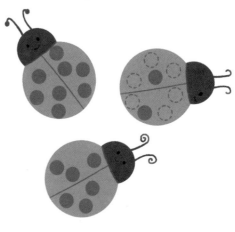

$3 \times 8 = ?$

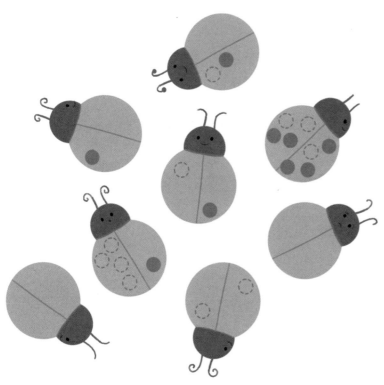

$8 \times 8 = ?$

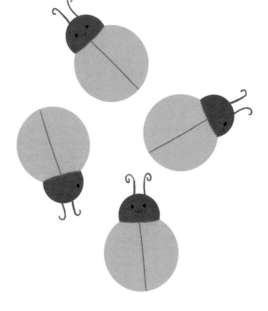

$4 \times 8 = ?$

Awesome Ants

Complete the multiplication by picking the right ant.

Fairy Fun

Draw in the missing fairies and work out the answer.

$$4 \times 4 = ?$$

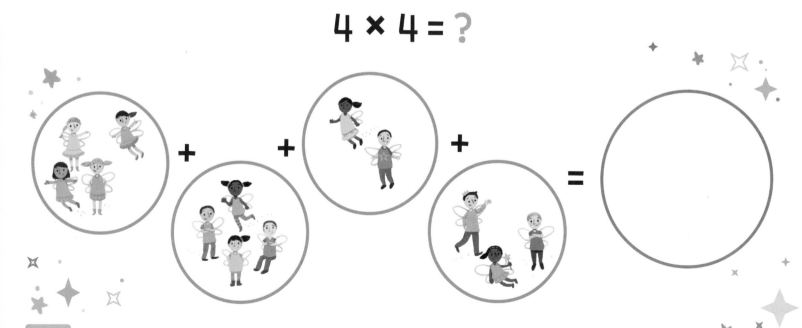

Robo-road

Help the robot collect the tools and get back to his friends.
You can only pick roads which are multiples of 4 or 8.

Test Your Knowledge

1) 4 x 2 = ?

2) 2 x 4 = ?

3) 3 x 4 = ?

4) 3 x 8 = ?

5) 5 x ? = 55

6) 5 x 12 = ?

7) 8 x 3 = ?

8) 4 x 3 = ?

9) 10 x 10 = ?

10) 10 x 5 = ?

Test Your Knowledge

1) 6 x 3 = ?

6) 6 x 4 = ?

2) ? x 4 = 20

7) 6 x 8 = ?

3) 7 x 8 = ?

8) 3 x ? = 30

4) 9 x 2 = ?

9) 3 x ? = 15

5) 2 x ? = 18

10) ? x 8 = 64

3 × Table

Wow! You've already learned your 2, 4, 5, 8, and 10 x tables.
Next up is the 3 x table!

1 × 3 = 3

2 × 3 = 6

3 × 3 = 9

4 × 3 = 12

5 × 3 = 15

6 × 3 = 18

7 × 3 = 21

8 × 3 = 24

9 × 3 = 27

10 × 3 = 30

11 × 3 = 33

12 × 3 = 36

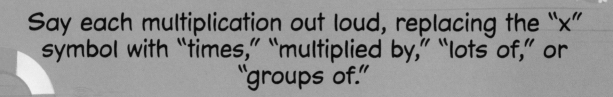

Say each multiplication out loud, replacing the "x" symbol with "times," "multiplied by," "lots of," or "groups of."

Fish Fill

Make sure there are the right number of fish in each bowl
to work out the correct answer!

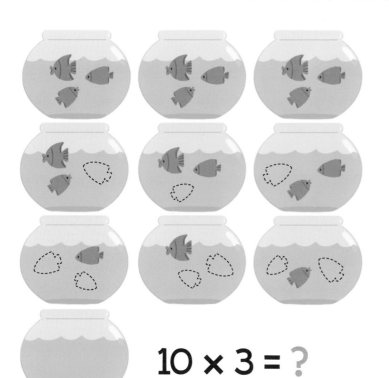

$$10 \times 3 = ?$$

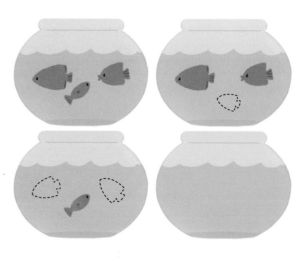

$$4 \times 3 = ?$$

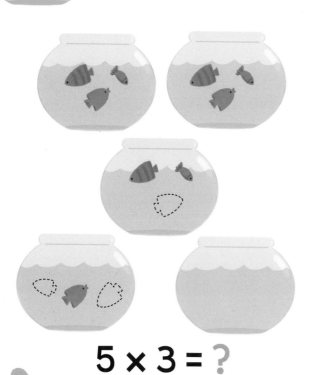

$$5 \times 3 = ?$$

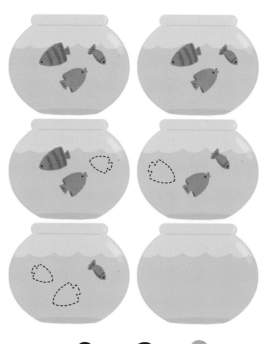

$$6 \times 3 = ?$$

Brick Build Up

Pick the correct brick to fill the space and complete the multiplication.

?

3	3	3	3

12
15
21
25

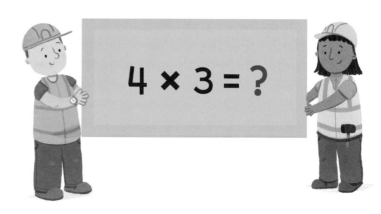

$$4 \times 3 = ?$$

Lost in Space!

Link each alien to the correct spaceship.

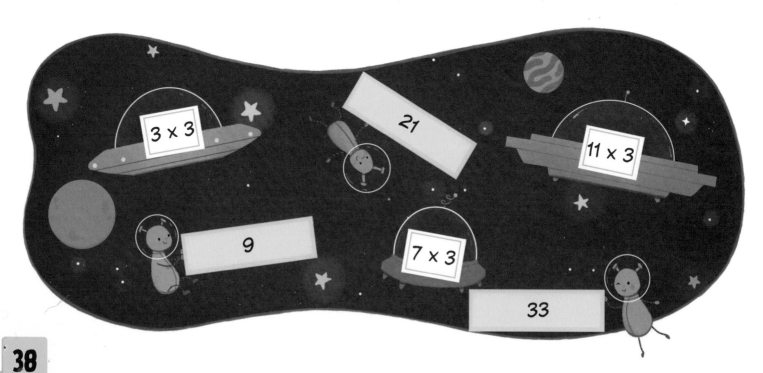

3 × 3

21

11 × 3

9

7 × 3

33

Underwater Wonderland

What are the fish trying to say?
Clue: Not all the letters in the key are needed!

_ N _ E _   _ _ E   _ E _
1   2   3   4 5   6 7

1) 3 X 4 = ?

3) 7 X 10 = ?

2) 5 X 6 = ?

4) 2 X 8 = ?

6) 8 X 4 = ?

7) 9 X 10 = ?

5) 3 X 7 = ?

KEY

60 = P	86 = Y	21 = H	90 = A	30 = D
44 = K	16 = T	32 = S	70 = R	12 = U

6 × Table

Now let's give the 6 x table a go. If you know the 3 x table, just *double* a *multiple* from the 3 x table to get the matching multiple in the 6 x table!

1 × 3 = 3   1 × 6 = 6   **Double** 3 **is** 6

2 × 3 = 6   2 × 6 = 12   **Double** 6 **is** 12

1 × 6 = 6	7 × 6 = 42
2 × 6 = 12	8 × 6 = 48
3 × 6 = 18	9 × 6 = 54
4 × 6 = 24	10 × 6 = 60
5 × 6 = 30	11 × 6 = 66
6 × 6 = 36	12 × 6 = 72

Say each multiplication out loud, replacing the "x" symbol with "times," "multiplied by," "lots of," or "groups of."

Busy Bugs

Make sure each bug has the correct number of spots and work out the answer to each multiplication.

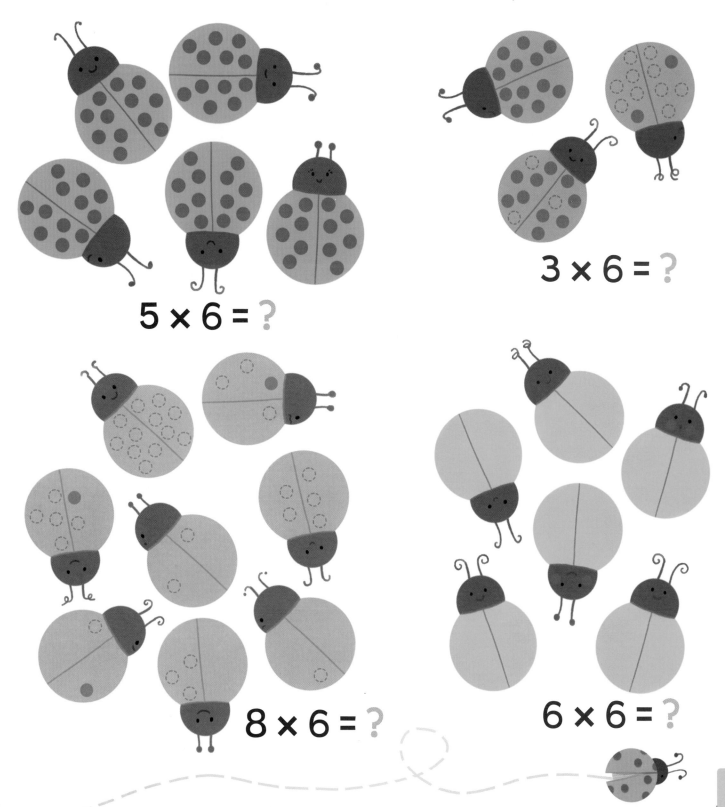

$5 \times 6 = ?$

$3 \times 6 = ?$

$8 \times 6 = ?$

$6 \times 6 = ?$

Pirate Pizza Party

Match each pirate up with the pizza they ordered.

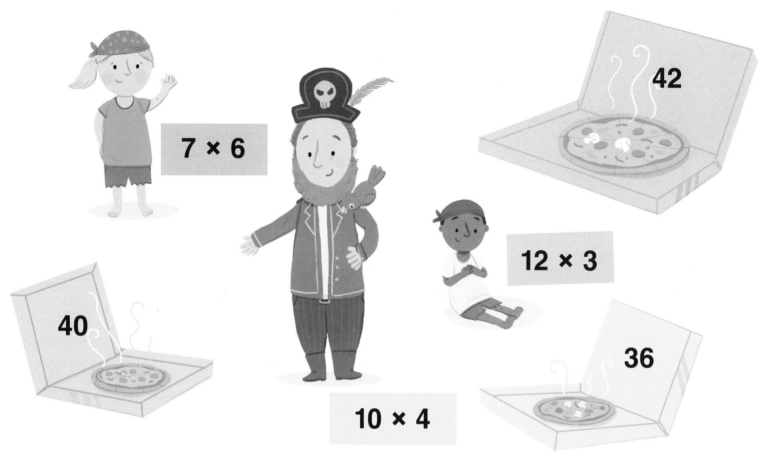

7×6

42

12×3

40

36

10×4

Busy Bees

Which numbers are the bees hiding?

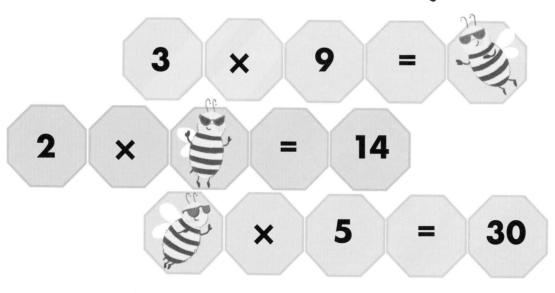

$3 \times 9 = $

$2 \times \ = 14$

$\ \times 5 = 30$

Creepy Crawly Maze

Help the worm get to his friends safely.

START HERE

$4 \times 6 = ?$ 24

28

$7 \times 3 = ?$ 21

40

25

$9 \times 5 = ?$

$8 \times 2 = ?$

16

45

36

72

FINISH

$11 \times 6 = ?$

66

Test Your Knowledge

1) 6 x 6 = ?

2) 5 x 6 = ?

3) 6 x 10 = ?

4) 4 x 4 = ?

5) 2 x 4 = ?

6) 8 x 4 = ?

7) 12 x 2 = ?

8) 6 x 2 = ?

9) 3 x 2 = ?

10) 3 x 4 = ?

Test Your Knowledge

1) 12 x 3 = ❓

2) 10 x 10 = ❓

3) 7 x 6 = ❓

4) 7 x 3 = ❓

5) 4 x 9 = ❓

6) 7 x 10 = ❓

7) 11 x 5 = ❓

8) 12 x 4 = ❓

9) 6 x 8 = ❓

10) 9 x 6 = ❓

9 × Table

Now we're ready for the 9 x table. For this one, it's useful to use the 10 x table and then subtract one lot of the number.

1 × 9 = 9	**7 × 9 = 63**
2 × 9 = 18	**8 × 9 = 72**
3 × 9 = 27	**9 × 9 = 81**
4 × 9 = 36	**10 × 9 = 90**
5 × 9 = 45	**11 × 9 = 99**
6 × 9 = 54	**12 × 9 = 108**

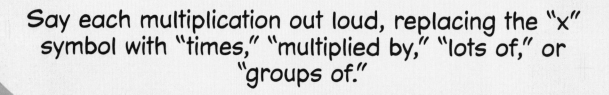

Say each multiplication out loud, replacing the "x" symbol with "times," "multiplied by," "lots of," or "groups of."

Times Table City Builder

Draw 9 windows in each tower to build your 9 x Table City!

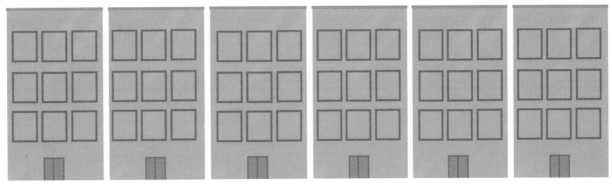

6 × 9 = ?

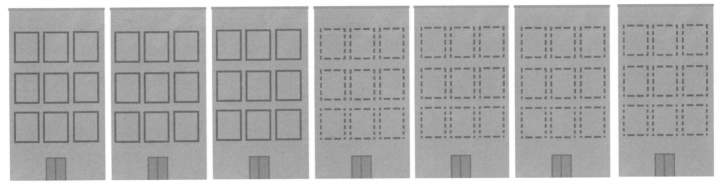

7 × 9 = ?

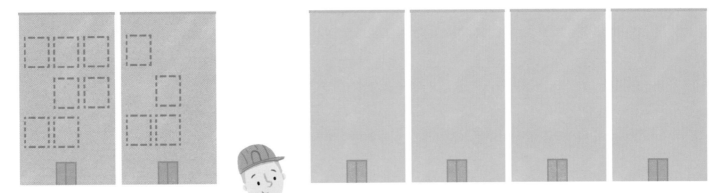

2 × 9 = ?

4 × 9 = ?

Spot the Dots

Which times table fact does the second group of giraffes show? Count the dots!

$$3 \times 9 = 27$$

$$\_ \times \_ = 27$$

Pyramid Puzzle

Use the mummy's clue to work out which tomb the explorer should visit.

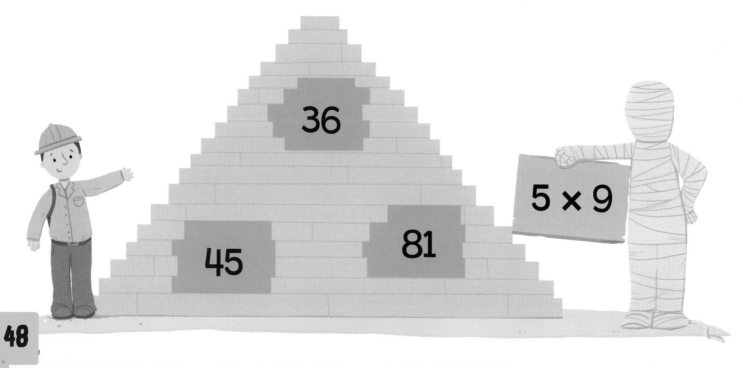

36

5 × 9

45   81

Zombie Run

Work out the secret spell to stop the zombies before it's too late!
Remember, not all the letters in the key are needed!

_ T _ _ _   _ _ _
1   23   4 5 6

1) 6 x 6   4) 5 x 5
2) 9 x 9   5) 10 x 10
3) 4 x 4   6) 3 x 3

KEY

36 = S   9 = L
100 = L   15 = B
16 = N   81 = U
25 = A   10 = Y

7 × Table

Some people think the 7 x table is hard, but the truth is you've already come across lots of multiples in it. You've done the hard work already!

$1 \times 7 = 7$

$2 \times 7 = 14$

$3 \times 7 = 21$

$4 \times 7 = 28$

$5 \times 7 = 35$

$6 \times 7 = 42$

$7 \times 7 = 49$

$8 \times 7 = 56$

$9 \times 7 = 63$

$10 \times 7 = 70$

$11 \times 7 = 77$

$12 \times 7 = 84$

Say each multiplication out loud, replacing the "x" symbol with "times," "multiplied by," "lots of," or "groups of."

Fish Fill

Make sure there are the right number of fish in each bowl to work out the correct answer!

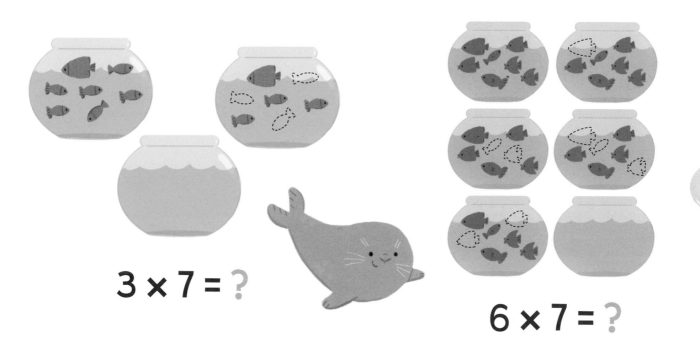

$3 \times 7 = ?$

$6 \times 7 = ?$

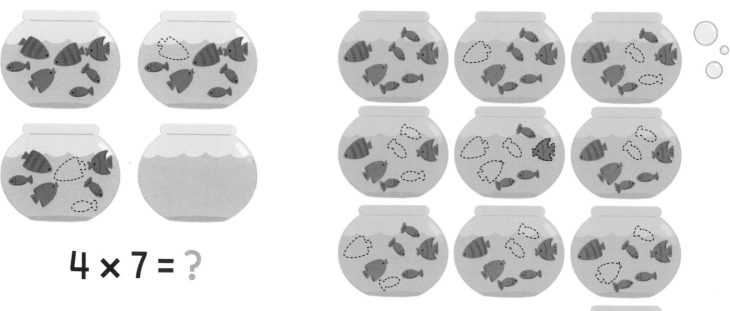

$4 \times 7 = ?$

$10 \times 7 = ?$

Shell Game

This tower follows the 7 x table. Who should go on top?

Penguin Picnic

Work out what times table fact the second picnic shows.

$7 \times 3 = 21$

$\_ \times \_ = 21$

Dino-roar

Fill in the dinosaur using the key below.

2 x 7 = ?   6 x 7 = ?   10 x 7 = ?   3 x 7 = ?   12 x 7 = ?

11 × Table

The 11 x table has a helpful pattern up until 9 x 11.

$$1 \times 11 = 11 \qquad 2 \times 11 = 22$$

$$3 \times 11 = 33$$

CAN YOU SPOT THE PATTERN?

1 × 11 = 11	7 × 11 = 77
2 × 11 = 22	8 × 11 = 88
3 × 11 = 33	9 × 11 = 99
4 × 11 = 44	10 × 11 = 110
5 × 11 = 55	11 × 11 = 121
6 × 11 = 66	12 × 11 = 132

Say each multiplication out loud,
replacing the "x" symbol with "times,"
"multiplied by," "lots of," or "groups of."

Times Table City Builder

Draw 11 windows in each tower to build your 11 x Table City!

$$5 \times 11 = ?$$

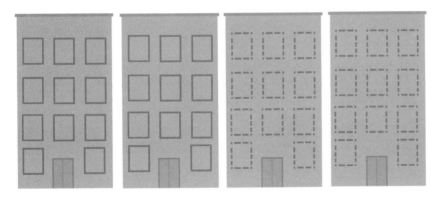
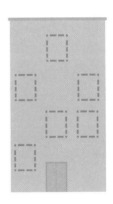

$$4 \times 11 = ?$$ $$1 \times 11 = ?$$

$$7 \times 11 = ?$$

Market Mix Up

Which bag has the wrong number of oranges?

$3 \times 11 = 33$

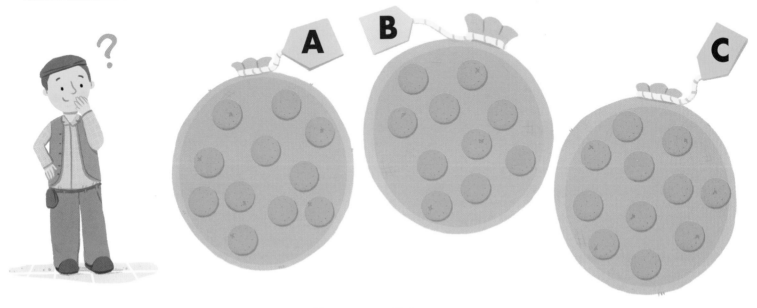

Line Up

Pick the guilty robber!

$= 12 \times 9$

18   90   108

Laundry Sort Out

Work out which item of clothing is the odd one out on each washing line.

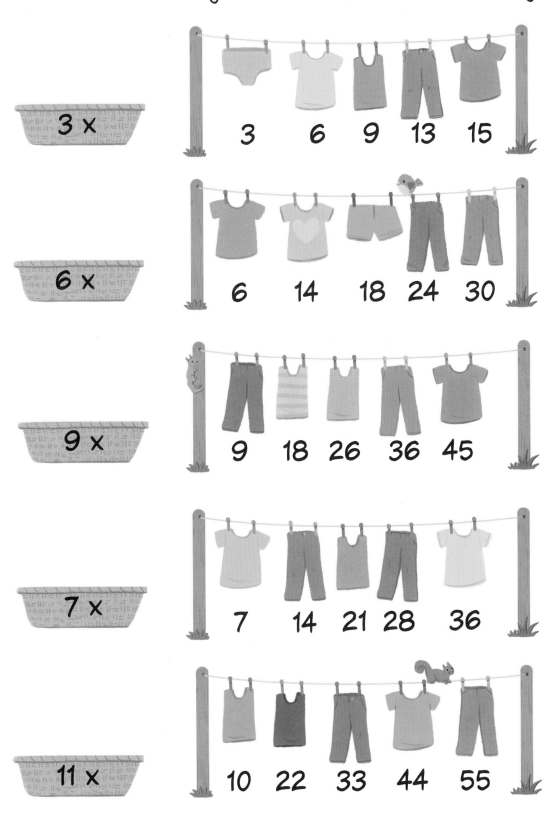

3 x

3   6   9   13   15

6 x

6   14   18   24   30

9 x

9   18   26   36   45

7 x

7   14   21   28   36

11 x

10   22   33   44   55

12 × Table

You've made it all the way to the final times table! Great work!
One last push and you will be a Times Table Pro!

1 × 12 = 12	7 × 12 = 84
2 × 12 = 24	8 × 12 = 96
3 × 12 = 36	9 × 12 = 108
4 × 12 = 48	10 × 12 = 120
5 × 12 = 60	11 × 12 = 132
6 × 12 = 72	12 × 12 = 144

Say each multiplication out loud, replacing the "x" symbol with "times," "multiplied by," "lots of," or "groups of."

Busy Bugs

Make sure each bug has the correct number of spots and work out the answer to each multiplication.

$$5 \times 12 = \text{?}$$

$$3 \times 12 = \text{?}$$

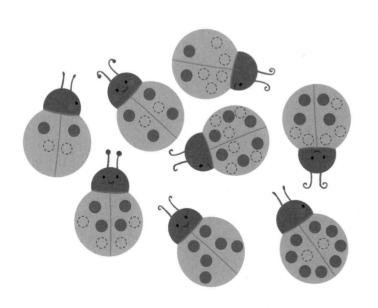

$$8 \times 12 = \text{?}$$

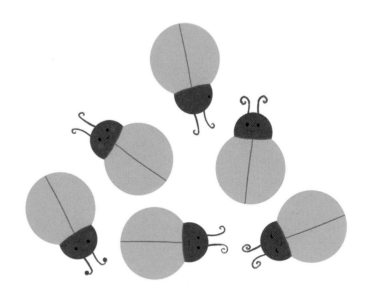

$$6 \times 12 = \text{?}$$

Missing Brick

Which brick should go on top?

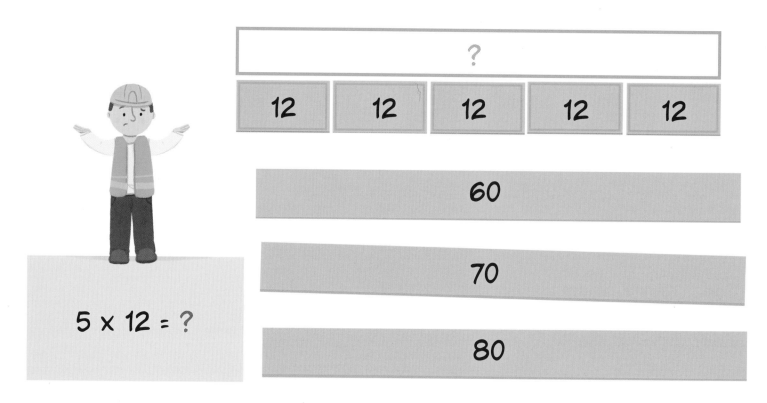

?

12	12	12	12	12

5 x 12 = ?

60

70

80

Bank Run

How much money is the pirate taking to the bank?
Count the amount in the bags and choose the correct total.

12

12   12

34   36   38

Light Up the Room

Help finish the stained glass window using the key below.

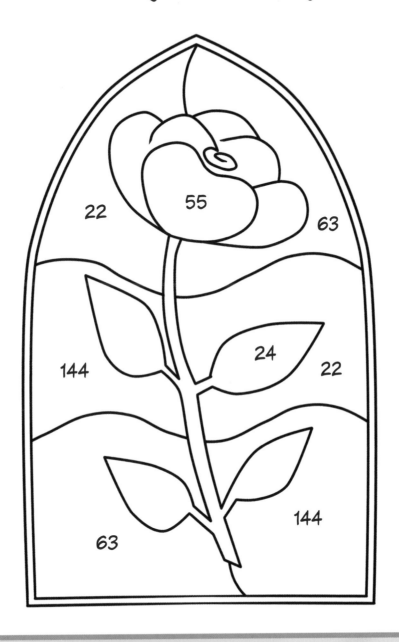

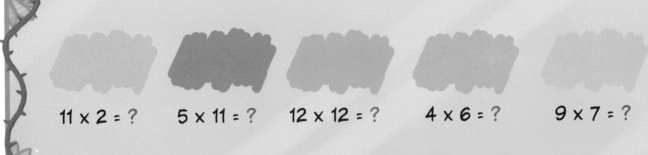

11 x 2 = ?   5 x 11 = ?   12 x 12 = ?   4 x 6 = ?   9 x 7 = ?

Test Your Knowledge

1) 2 x 12 = ?

2) 2 x 6 = ?

3) 2 x 3 = ?

4) 4 x 12 = ?

5) 4 x 6 = ?

6) 4 x 3 = ?

7) 9 x 10 = ?

8) 9 x 9 = ?

9) 8 x 7 = ?

10) 7 x 8 = ?

Test Your Knowledge

1) 3 x 12 = ☐ ?

2) 9 x 8 = ☐ ?

3) 10 x 12 = ☐ ?

4) 3 x 8 = ☐ ?

5) 7 x 7 = ☐ ?

6) 6 x 7 = ☐ ?

7) 4 x 8 = ☐ ?

8) 3 x 10 = ☐ ?

9) 12 x 11 = ☐ ?

10) 8 x 8 = ☐ ?

Division: Sharing

Division is the opposite of multiplication. We can think of division as sharing an amount into equal groups.

(10) ÷ (5) = ?

Let's share 10 apples into 5 bowls equally. We can move each apple one by one until we have used all the apples. How many apples are there in each bowl/equal group?

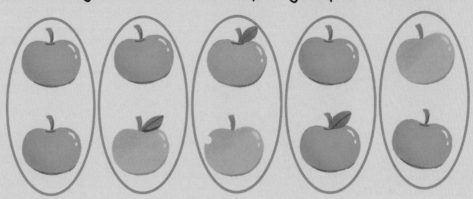

(10) ÷ (5) = 2

Banana Split

How many bananas does each monkey get?

(6) ÷ (2) = ?

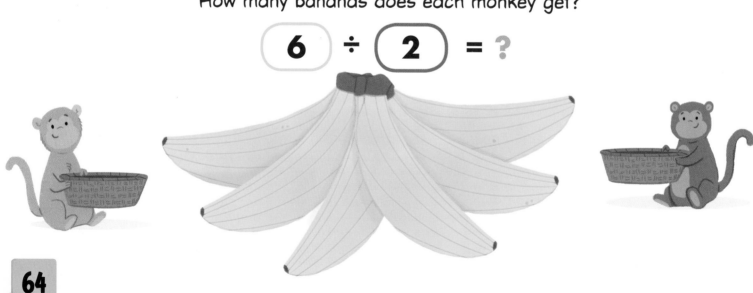

Cavalry Crevasse

How many horses are on each side of the crack?

$$12 \div 2 = \text{?}$$

Jail Run

How many robbers will end up in each jail?

$$15 \div 3 = \text{?}$$

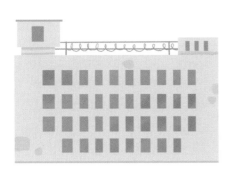

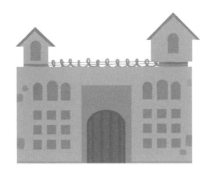

Mermaids' Treasure

Share the jewels out equally between each mermaid. How many does each one get?

$$15 \div 5 = \text{?}$$

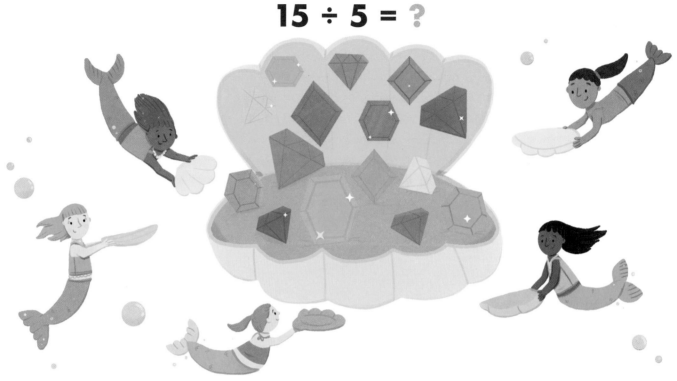

Beakfast!

How many worms does each chick get for breakfast?

$$8 \div 4 = \text{?}$$

Pixie Palace

Help decorate the palace using the key below.

$6 \div 3 = ?$ $20 \div 2 = ?$ $8 \div 2 = ?$ $15 \div 3 = ?$ $24 \div 2 = ?$

Working Out the Inverse

Another way of saying that division and multiplication are opposites is that they are *inverse* of each other. You can have fun working out the inverse of number sentences.

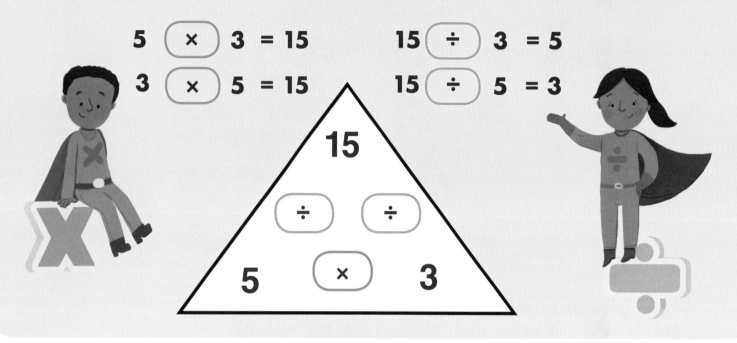

$5 \times 3 = 15$ $15 \div 3 = 5$

$3 \times 5 = 15$ $15 \div 5 = 3$

15

$\div$ $\div$

5     $\times$ 3

Pyramid Puzzle

Use the Super Inverse Triangle inside the pyramid to help you fill in the gaps!

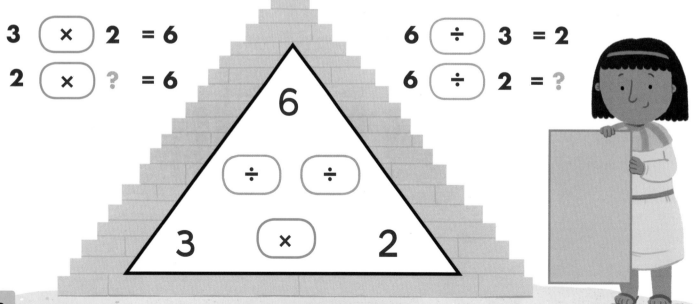

$3 \times 2 = 6$ $6 \div 3 = 2$

$2 \times ? = 6$ $6 \div 2 = ?$

6

$\div$ $\div$

3     $\times$ 2

Goblin Gold

Share the coins equally among the goblins. Can you write the two inverse equations? Use the Super Inverse Triangle to help you.

$$20 \div 5 = \text{?}$$

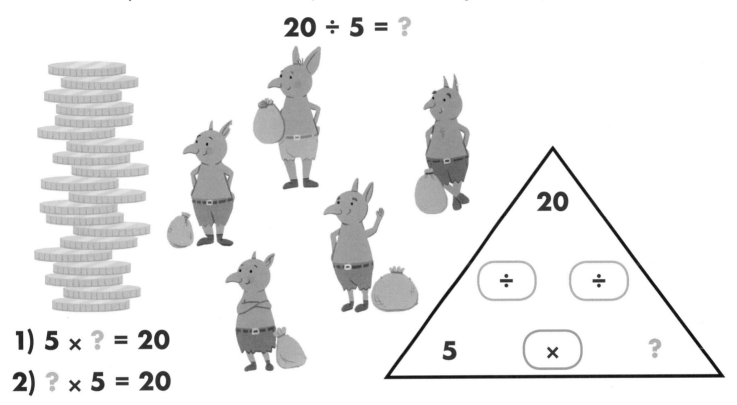

1) $5 \times \text{?} = 20$

2) $\text{?} \times 5 = 20$

Treetop Tightrope

Which rope leads the monkey to the correct inverse number sentence?

$5 \div 3 = 15$

$3 \div 5 = 15$

$3 \times 5 = \text{?}$

$15 \div 3 = 5$

Odd and Even Numbers

With **even** numbers you can always share them out equally between two groups.

With **odd** numbers, one group always gets more and one always gets less!

All Aboard

Work out if the number of penguins waiting to board the two boats is odd or even.

Spring Clean

Help the fairy tidy up all the odd and even numbers into the right boxes.

Odd Dinner

Which clown is the odd one out?

Division: Grouping

Another way of thinking about division is *grouping*.
How many groups of 2 gloves can you make from 10?

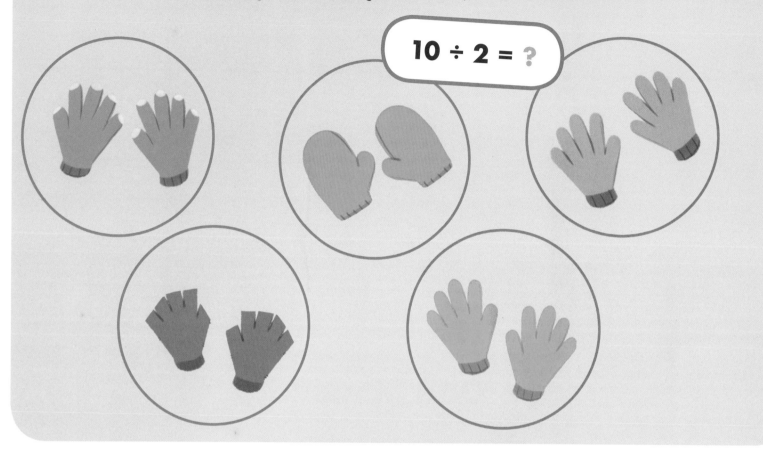

10 ÷ 2 = ?

Coop Count Up

12 ÷ 6 = ?

How many groups of 6 eggs can you make?

Monster Mechanics

How many groups of 4 wheels can you make?

$$16 \div 4 = \text{?}$$

Spider Slippers

How many groups of 8 slippers does the spider have?

$$24 \div 8 = \text{?}$$

Mount Mushroom

How many mushrooms will each pig carry back home if they share them equally?

$$18 \div 3 = \text{?}$$

Pony Party

How many horseshoes are needed?

$$5 \times 4 = \text{?}$$

Wild Goose Race

Help the goose get to the finish line!

START HERE

$20 \div 2 = ?$

10

2

14

$15 \div 5 = ?$

3

10

$14 \div 7 = ?$

2

2

$3 \times 3 = ?$

6

35

$7 \times 7 = ?$

49

HOME

Market Mix-up

Match the total of each number sentence to the correct food.

$5 \times 2 = ?$

$24 \div 4 = ?$

$40 \div 10 = ?$

Honeycomb Hunt

Which segment is missing?

14 ÷ = 2

7   12   5

Boar-thday Cake

How many slices of cake will each boar get?
Complete the number sentence below.

$$6 \div \_ = \_$$

Oh Mummy!

Fill in the sarcophagus after solving the key below.

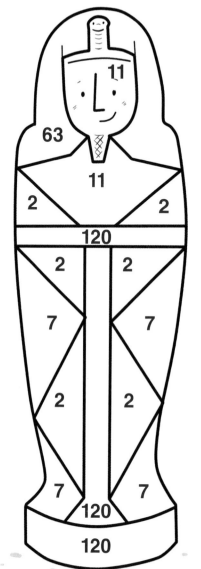

$22 \div 2 = ?$ $12 \times 10 = ?$ $21 \div 3 = ?$ $7 \times 9 = ?$ $10 \div 5 = ?$

Friends from Afar

What are the aliens trying to say to you?
Find the solutions and use the key to work it out.

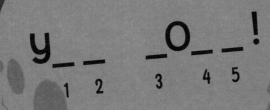

y_ _ _ _O_ _ !
 1 2 3 4 5

1) 12 x 12 = ?

2) 33 ÷ 3 = ?

3) 9 x 7 = ?

4) 35 ÷ 7 = ?

5) 10 x 1 = ?

KEY

11 = U	81 = D	25 = B
5 = C	63 = R	10 = K
144= O	90= Y	

Test Your Knowledge

See how long it takes you to fill in the blanks.

×	1	2	3	4	5	6	7	8	9	10	11	12
1	1											
2		4										
3			9									
4				16								
5					25							
6						36						
7							49					
8								64				
9									81			
10										100		
11											121	
12												144

Test Your Knowledge

1) 6 × 3 = ☐

2) 18 ÷ 3 = ☐

3) 7 × 7 = ☐

4) 49 ÷ 7 = ☐

5) 16 ÷ 4 = ☐

6) 4 × 4 = ☐

7) 5 × 6 = ☐

8) 6 × 5 = ☐

9) 30 ÷ 5 = ☐

10) 30 ÷ 6 = ☐

Test Your Knowledge

See how long it takes you to fill in the blanks.

×	1	4	6	10	2	5	7	11	9	3	8	12
1	1	4		10		5			9		8	
2			12		4			22		6		
3		12			6	15	21			9		
4					8	20			36			48
5		20				25	35				40	
6					12			66		18		72
7			42			35		77			56	
8		32			16					24		
9				90					81			
10												
11							77					132
12			72						108			

Test Your Knowledge

1) Circle the odd numbers: | 12 33 54 2 91 |

2) Circle the even numbers: | 21 11 32 1,000 |

3) 40 ÷ 5 = ☐

4) 45 ÷ 5 = ☐

5) 20 ÷ 4 = ☐

6) 9 × 12 = ☐

7) 12 × 10 = ☐

8) 7 × 8 = ☐

9) 6 × 9 = ☐

10) 9 = 81 ÷ ☐

Test Your Knowledge

See how long it takes you to fill in the blanks.

×	1	4	6	10	2	5	7	11	9	3	8	12
1	1	4		10	5				9		8	
2			12		4			22		6		
3		12			6	15	21					
4					8				36			
5		20									40	
6					12			66		18		72
7			42			35					56	
8		32			16					24		
9				90					81			
10												
11							77					132
12			72									

Test Your Knowledge

1) $3 \times 12 =$ ☐

2) $6 \times 12 =$ ☐

3) $2 \times 5 =$ ☐

4) $4 \times 5 =$ ☐

5) $8 \times 5 =$ ☐

6) $72 = 9 \times$ ☐

7) $64 \div 8 =$ ☐

8) $50 = 5 \times$ ☐

9) $12 \times 7 =$ ☐

10) $54 \div 9 =$ ☐

Test Your Knowledge

See how long it takes you to fill in the blanks.

×	1	4	6	10	2	5	7	11	9	3	8	12
1												
2												
3												
4												
5												
6												
7												
8												
9												
10												
11												
12												

Test Your Knowledge

1) Miss Tunch shares 20 chocolates equally among 5 children. How many chocolates does each child get?

2) 10 coins are split equally into 5 bags. How many coins are in each bag?

3) 24 animals need to split into groups of two. How many groups of 2 will there be?

4) 10 aliens have two zappers each. How many zappers do they have altogether?

5) Each sleigh needs 6 reindeer. If there are 6 sleighs, how many reindeer are needed?

Test Your Knowledge

See how long it takes you to fill in the blanks.

×	2	5	7	9	10	1	3	8	12	4	11	6
6												
3												
1												
9												
10												
4												
7												
5												
12												
2												
8												
11												

Test Your Knowledge

1) 30 children split into 3 equal teams. How many children will be in each team?

2) There are 4 cats. Each cat has 5 kittens. How many kittens are there altogether?

3) A wizard sorts his 15 wands into 5 drawers. How many wands will end up in each drawer?

4) There are 4 buses for a school trip. Each bus can take 6 children. How many children can go on the school trip?

5) There are 7 pirates who discover a treasure chest with 42 rubies. How many rubies does each pirate get, if they share them equally?

Solutions

Page 5 — Machine Mix-up

MULTIPLICATION
1 Multiplied by
2 Times
3 Lots of
4 Groups of

DIVISION
1 Divided by
2 Sharing
3 Grouping

Page 6 — Missing Numbers

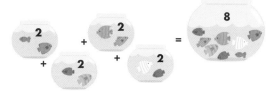

Page 7 — Monkey Match Up

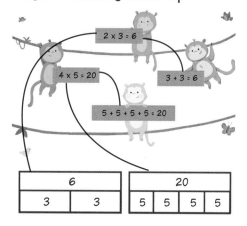

$2 \times 3 = 6$

$4 \times 5 = 20$

$3 + 3 = 6$

$5 + 5 + 5 + 5 = 20$

6
3	3

20
5	5	5	5

Page 9 — Times Table City Builder

$3 \times 10 = \boxed{30}$ $5 \times 10 = \boxed{50}$
$2 \times 10 = \boxed{20}$ $4 \times 10 = \boxed{40}$

Page 10 — Missing Marbles

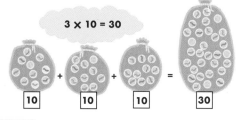

$3 \times 10 = 30$

10 10 10 30

Page 10 — Seal Conceal

$2 \times 10 = \boxed{20}$ $\boxed{12} \times 10 = 120$
$4 \times \boxed{10} = 40$

Page 11 — Wild, Wild West

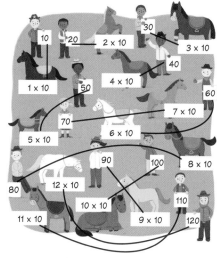

10 20 2 × 10 30 3 × 10
40 1 × 10 50 4 × 10 60
70 7 × 10 5 × 10 6 × 10
90 100 8 × 10 80 12 × 10
10 × 10 110 11 × 10 9 × 10 120

Page 13 — Busy Bugs

$2 \times 2 = \boxed{4}$ $4 \times 2 = \boxed{8}$
$7 \times 2 = \boxed{14}$ $5 \times 2 = \boxed{10}$

Page 14 — Pixie Party

$5 \times \boxed{2} = 10$ $9 \times 2 = \boxed{18}$
$\boxed{10} \times 2 = 20$

Page 14 — Spot the Mistake

$4 \times 2 = 8$

Page 15 — Superhero Sort Out

Page 17 — Fish Fill

$6 \times 5 = \boxed{30}$ $9 \times 5 = \boxed{45}$
$5 \times 5 = \boxed{25}$ $7 \times 5 = \boxed{35}$

Page 18 — Safari Sun

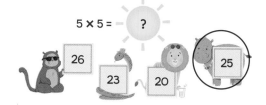

$5 \times 5 = \boxed{?}$

26 23 20 25

Page 18 — Balloon Brigade

$3 \times 5 = \boxed{15}$ $\boxed{10} \times 5 = 50$
$8 \times \boxed{5} = 40$

Solutions

Page 19   Showtime

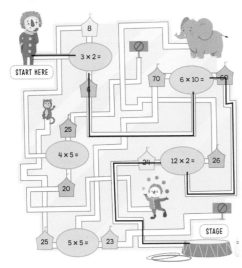

Page 20   Test Your Knowledge

1) 4	6) 70
2) 6	7) 100
3) 20	8) 110
4) 25	9) 120
5) 60	10) 10

Page 21   Test Your Knowledge

1) 12	6) 90
2) 18	7) 30
3) 10	8) 20
4) 35	9) 24
5) 40	10) 55

Page 22   Goblin Gruel

$10 \times \boxed{2} = 20$

Page 23   Hop To It!

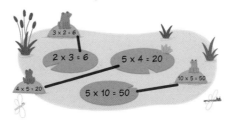

Page 23   Number Machine

1) $4 \times 3 = 12$
2) $7 \times 2 = 14$
3) $5 \times 6 = 30$

Page 24   Fish Fun

1) $5 + 5 = 10$
2) $2 + 2 + 2 + 2 + 2 = 10$

Page 24   Hat Swap

1) $4 + 4 + 4 = 12$
2) $3 + 3 + 3 + 3 = 12$

Page 25   Pirate Portrait

Page 27   Times Table City Builder

1) $4 \times 4 = 16$ 3) $9 \times 4 = 36$
2) $6 \times 4 = 24$ 4) $5 \times 4 = 20$

Page 28   Dino Dinner

$3 \times \boxed{4} = \boxed{12}$

Page 28   Under the Sea

$6 \times 4 = 24$

Page 29   Knight Time!

Page 31   Busy Bugs

1) $2 \times 8 = 16$
2) $3 \times 8 = 24$
3) $8 \times 8 = 64$
4) $4 \times 8 = 32$

Page 32   Awesome Ants

$5 \times \boxed{8} = 40$

Page 32   Fairy Fun

$4 \times 4 = 16$

Solutions

Page 33 Robo-road

Page 34 Test Your Knowledge

1) 8
2) 8
3) 12
4) 24
5) 11
6) 60
7) 24
8) 12
9) 100
10) 50

Page 35 Test Your Knowledge

1) 18
2) 5
3) 56
4) 18
5) 9
6) 24
7) 48
8) 10
9) 5
10) 8

Page 37 Fish Fill

1) 10 × 3 = 30
2) 4 × 3 = 12
3) 5 × 3 = 15
4) 6 × 3 = 18

Page 38 Brick Build Up

4 × 3 = 12

Page 38 Lost in Space!

Page 39 Underwater Wonderland

UNDER THE SEA

1) 3 × 4 = 12
2) 5 × 6 = 30
3) 7 × 10 = 70
4) 2 × 8 = 16
5) 3 × 7 = 21
6) 8 × 4 = 32
7) 9 × 10 = 90

Page 41 Busy Bugs

1) 5 × 6 = 30
2) 3 × 6 = 18
3) 8 × 6 = 48
4) 6 × 6 = 36

Page 42 Pirate Pizza Party

Page 42 Busy Bees

3 × 9 = (27)
2 × (7) = 14
(6) × 5 = 30

Page 43 Creepy Crawly Maze

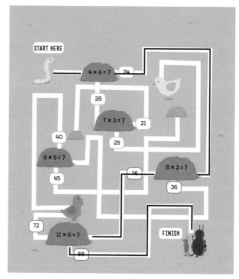

Page 44 Test Your Knowledge

1) 36
2) 30
3) 60
4) 16
5) 8
6) 32
7) 24
8) 12
9) 6
10) 12

Page 45 Test Your Knowledge

1) 36
2) 100
3) 42
4) 21
5) 36
6) 70
7) 55
8) 48
9) 48
10) 54

Solutions

Page 47   Times Table City Builder
1) 6 × 9 = 54
2) 7 × 9 = 63
3) 2 × 9 = 18
4) 4 × 9 = 36

Page 48   Spot the Dots

⬭9⬭ × ⬭3⬭ = 27

Page 48   Pyramid Puzzle

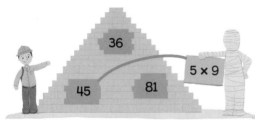

Page 49   Zombie Run

STUN ALL

1) 6 × 6 = 36   4) 5 × 5 = 25
2) 9 × 9 = 81   5) 10 × 10 = 100
3) 4 × 4 = 16   6) 3 × 3 = 9

Page 51   Fish Fill
1) 3 × 7 = 21
2) 6 × 7 = 42
3) 4 × 7 = 28
4) 10 × 7 = 70

Page 52   Shell Game
28

Page 52   Penguin Picnic
3 × 7 = 21

Page 53   Dino-roar

Page 55   Times Table City Builder
1) 5 × 11 = 55
2) 4 × 11 = 44
3) 1 × 11 = 11
4) 7 × 11 = 77

Page 56   Market Mix-up
B has only 10 oranges

Page 56   Line Up
Robber C
108 = 12 × 9

Page 57   Laundry Sort Out

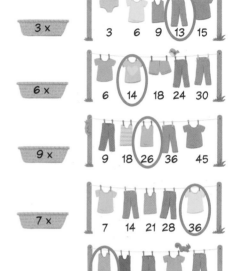

Page 59   Busy Bugs
1) 5 × 12 = 60
2) 3 × 12 = 36
3) 8 × 12 = 96
4) 6 × 12 = 72

Page 60   Missing Brick
1) 5 × 12 = 60

Page 60   Bank Run

Solutions

Page 61   Light Up the Room

Page 62   Test Your Knowledge

1) 24   6) 12
2) 12   7) 90
3) 6   8) 81
4) 48   9) 56
5) 24   10) 56

Page 63   Test Your Knowledge

1) 36   6) 42
2) 72   7) 32
3) 120   8) 30
4) 24   9) 132
5) 49   10) 64

Page 64   Banana Split

$6 \div 2 = 3$

Page 65   Cavalry Crevasse

$12 \div 2 = 6$

Page 65   Jail Run

$15 \div 3 = 5$

Page 66   Mermaids' Treasure

$15 \div 5 = 3$

Page 66   Beakfast!

$8 \div 4 = 2$

Page 67   Pixie Palace

Page 68   Pyramid Puzzle

1) $2 \times 3 = 6$
2) $6 \div 2 = 3$

Page 69   Goblin Gold

1) $20 \div 5 = 4$
2) $5 \times 4 = 20$
3) $4 \times 5 = 20$

Page 69   Treetop Tightrope

$15 \div 3 = 5$

Page 70   Odd and Even Numbers

1) 4 is even
2) 5 is odd

Page 70   All Aboard

11 is odd

Page 71   Spring Clean

Page 71   Odd Dinner

Solutions

Page 72   Division: Grouping

$10 \div 2 = 5$

Page 72   Coop Count Up

$12 \div 6 = 2$

Page 73   Monster Mechanics

$16 \div 4 = 4$

Page 73   Spider Slippers

$24 \div 8 = 3$

Page 74   Mount Mushroom

$18 \div 3 = 6$

Page 74   Pony Party

$5 \times 4 = 20$

Page 75   Wild Goose Race

Page 76   Market Mix-up

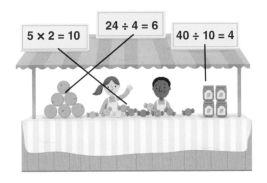

Page 76   Honeycomb Hunt

Page 77   Boar-thday Cake

$6 \div \boxed{3} = \boxed{2}$

Page 78   Oh Mummy!

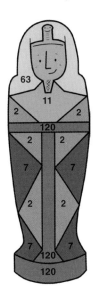

Page 79   Friends from Afar

YOU ROCK!

1) $12 \times 12 = 144$ 4) $35 \div 7 = 5$

2) $33 \div 3 = 11$ 5) $10 \times 1 = 10$

3) $9 \times 7 = 63$

Page 80   Test Your Knowledge

×	1	2	3	4	5	6	7	8	9	10	11	12
1	1	2	3	4	5	6	7	8	9	10	11	12
2	2	4	6	8	10	12	14	16	18	20	22	24
3	3	6	9	12	15	18	21	24	27	30	33	36
4	4	8	12	16	20	24	28	32	36	40	44	48
5	5	10	15	20	25	30	35	40	45	50	55	60
6	6	12	18	24	30	36	42	48	54	60	66	72
7	7	14	21	28	35	42	49	56	63	70	77	84
8	8	16	24	32	40	48	56	64	72	80	88	96
9	9	18	27	36	45	54	63	72	81	90	99	108
10	10	20	30	40	50	60	70	80	90	100	110	120
11	11	22	33	44	55	66	77	88	99	110	121	132
12	12	24	36	48	60	72	84	96	108	120	132	144

Page 81   Test Your Knowledge

1) 18   6) 16

2) 6   7) 30

3) 49   8) 30

4) 7   9) 6

5) 4   10) 5

Solutions

Page 82 Test Your Knowledge

×	1	4	6	10	2	5	7	11	9	3	8	12
1	1	4	6	10	2	5	7	11	9	3	8	12
2	2	8	12	20	4	10	14	22	18	6	16	24
3	3	12	18	30	6	15	21	33	27	9	24	36
4	4	16	24	40	8	20	28	44	36	12	32	48
5	5	20	30	50	10	25	35	55	45	15	40	60
6	6	24	36	60	12	30	42	66	54	18	48	72
7	7	28	42	70	14	35	49	77	63	21	56	84
8	8	32	48	80	16	40	56	88	72	24	64	96
9	9	36	54	90	18	45	63	99	81	27	72	108
10	10	40	60	100	20	50	70	110	90	30	80	120
11	11	44	66	110	22	55	77	121	99	33	88	132
12	12	48	72	120	24	60	84	132	108	36	96	144

Page 83 Test Your Knowledge

1) 33, 91
2) 32; 1,000
3) 8
4) 9
5) 5
6) 108
7) 120
8) 56
9) 54
10) 9

Page 84 Test Your Knowledge

×	1	4	6	10	2	5	7	11	9	3	8	12
1	1	4	6	10	2	5	7	11	9	3	8	12
2	2	8	12	20	4	10	14	22	18	6	16	24
3	3	12	18	30	6	15	21	33	27	9	24	36
4	4	16	24	40	8	20	28	44	36	12	32	48
5	5	20	30	50	10	25	35	55	45	15	40	60
6	6	24	36	60	12	30	42	66	54	18	48	72
7	7	28	42	70	14	35	49	77	63	21	56	84
8	8	32	48	80	16	40	56	88	72	24	64	96
9	9	36	54	90	18	45	63	99	81	27	72	108
10	10	40	60	100	20	50	70	110	90	30	80	120
11	11	44	66	110	22	55	77	121	99	33	88	132
12	12	48	72	120	24	60	84	132	108	36	96	144

Page 85 Test Your Knowledge

1) 36
2) 72
3) 10
4) 20
5) 40
6) 8
7) 8
8) 10
9) 84
10) 6

Page 86 Test Your Knowledge

×	1	4	6	10	2	5	7	11	9	3	8	12
1	1	4	6	10	2	5	7	11	9	3	8	12
2	2	8	12	20	4	10	14	22	18	6	16	24
3	3	12	18	30	6	15	21	33	27	9	24	36
4	4	16	24	40	8	20	28	44	36	12	32	48
5	5	20	30	50	10	25	35	55	45	15	40	60
6	6	24	36	60	12	30	42	66	54	18	48	72
7	7	28	42	70	14	35	49	77	63	21	56	84
8	8	32	48	80	16	40	56	88	72	24	64	96
9	9	36	54	90	18	45	63	99	81	27	72	108
10	10	40	60	100	20	50	70	110	90	30	80	120
11	11	44	66	110	22	55	77	121	99	33	88	132
12	12	48	72	120	24	60	84	132	108	36	96	144

Page 87 Test Your Knowledge

1) 4
2) 2
3) 12
4) 20
5) 36

Page 88 Test Your Knowledge

×	2	5	7	9	10	1	3	8	12	4	11	6
6	12	30	35	54	60	6	18	48	72	24	66	36
3	6	15	21	27	30	3	9	24	36	12	33	18
1	2	5	7	9	10	1	3	8	12	4	11	6
9	18	45	63	81	90	9	27	72	108	36	99	54
10	20	50	70	90	100	10	30	80	120	40	110	60
4	8	20	28	36	40	4	12	32	48	16	44	24
7	14	35	49	63	70	7	21	56	84	28	77	42
5	10	25	35	45	50	5	15	40	60	20	55	30
12	24	60	84	108	120	12	36	96	144	48	132	72
2	4	10	14	18	20	2	6	16	24	8	22	12
8	16	40	56	72	80	8	24	64	96	32	88	48
11	22	55	77	99	110	11	33	88	132	44	121	66

Page 89 Test Your Knowledge

1) 10
2) 20
3) 3
4) 24
5) 6